Happy Easter!
This belongs to:

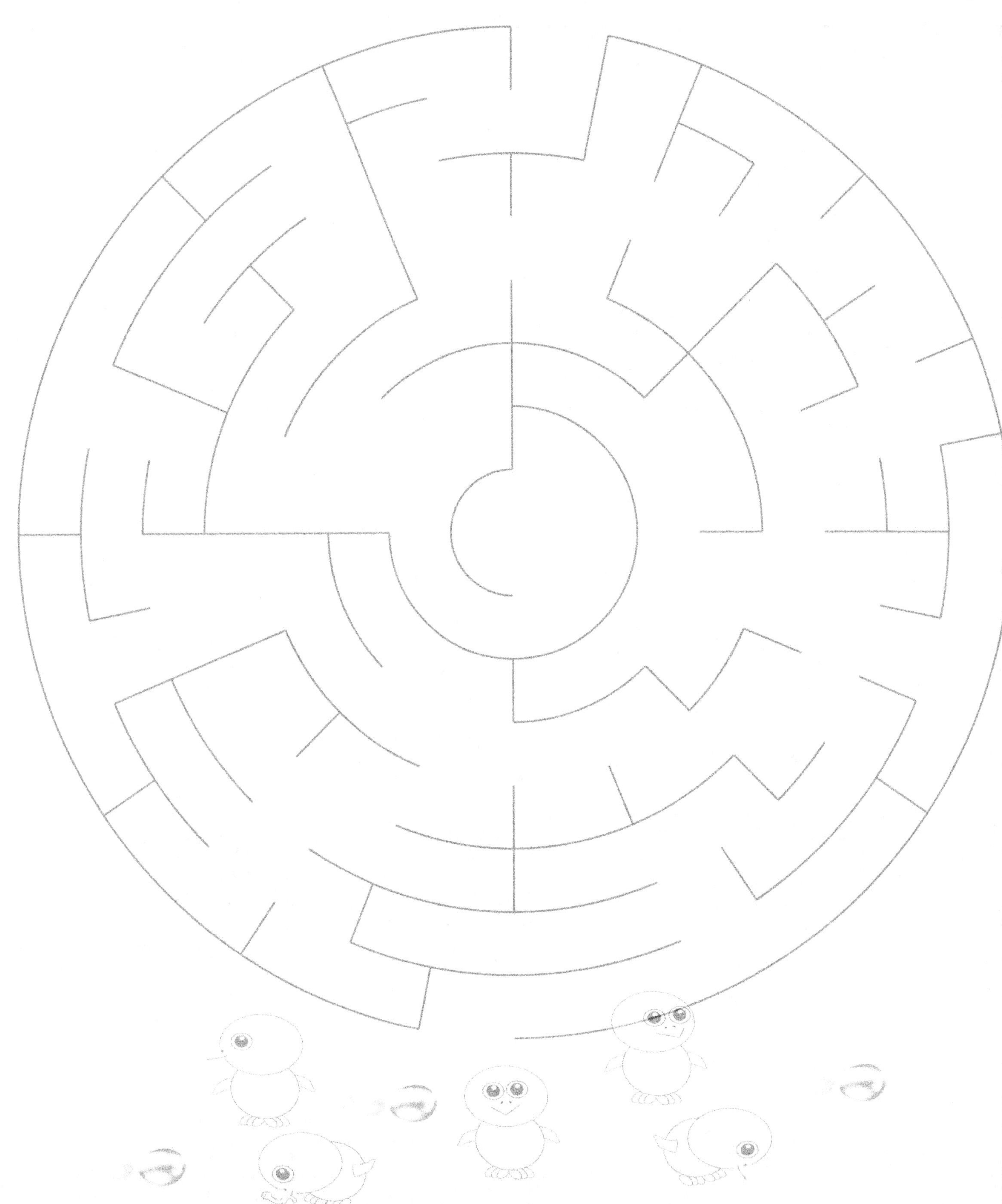

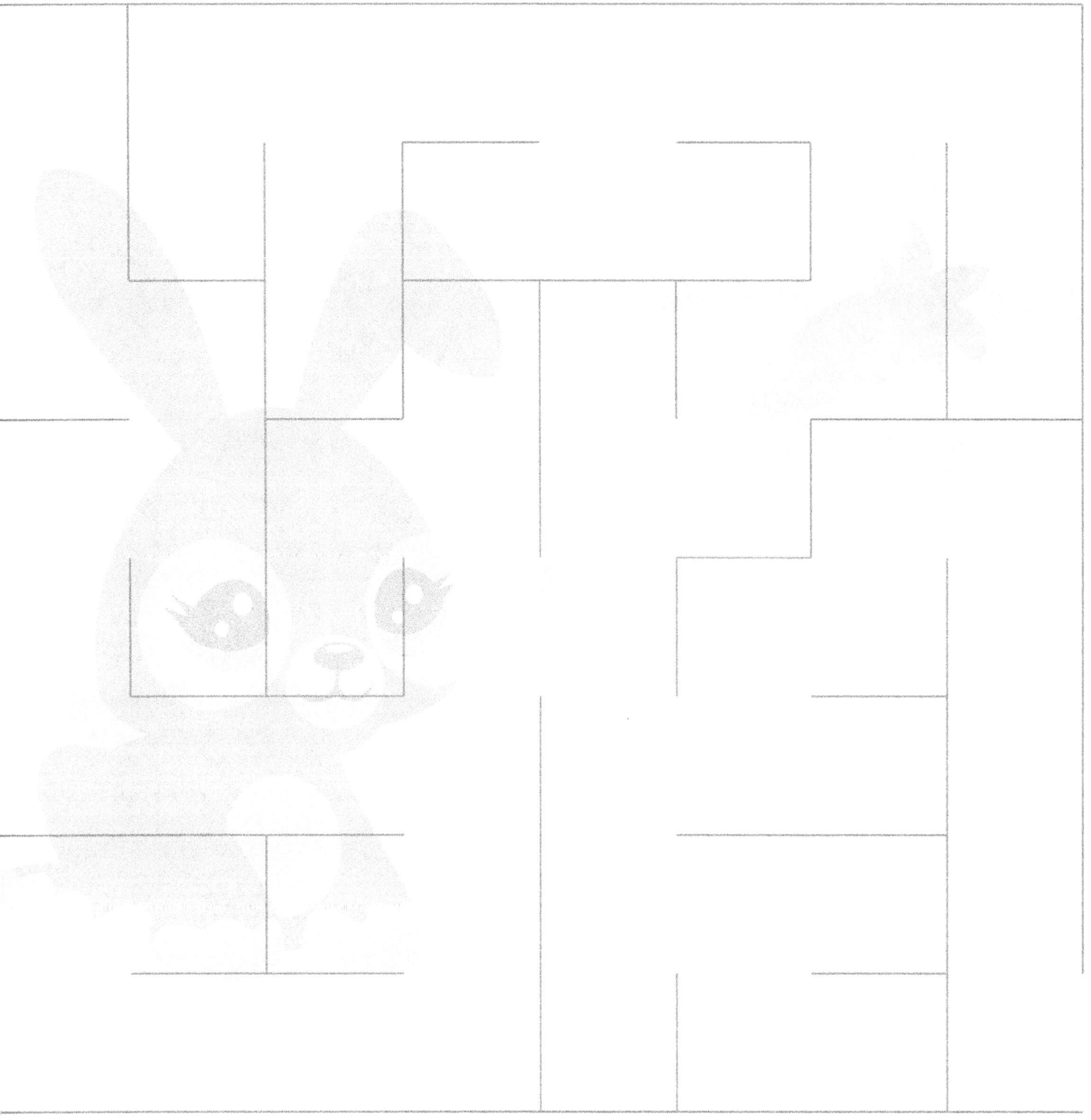

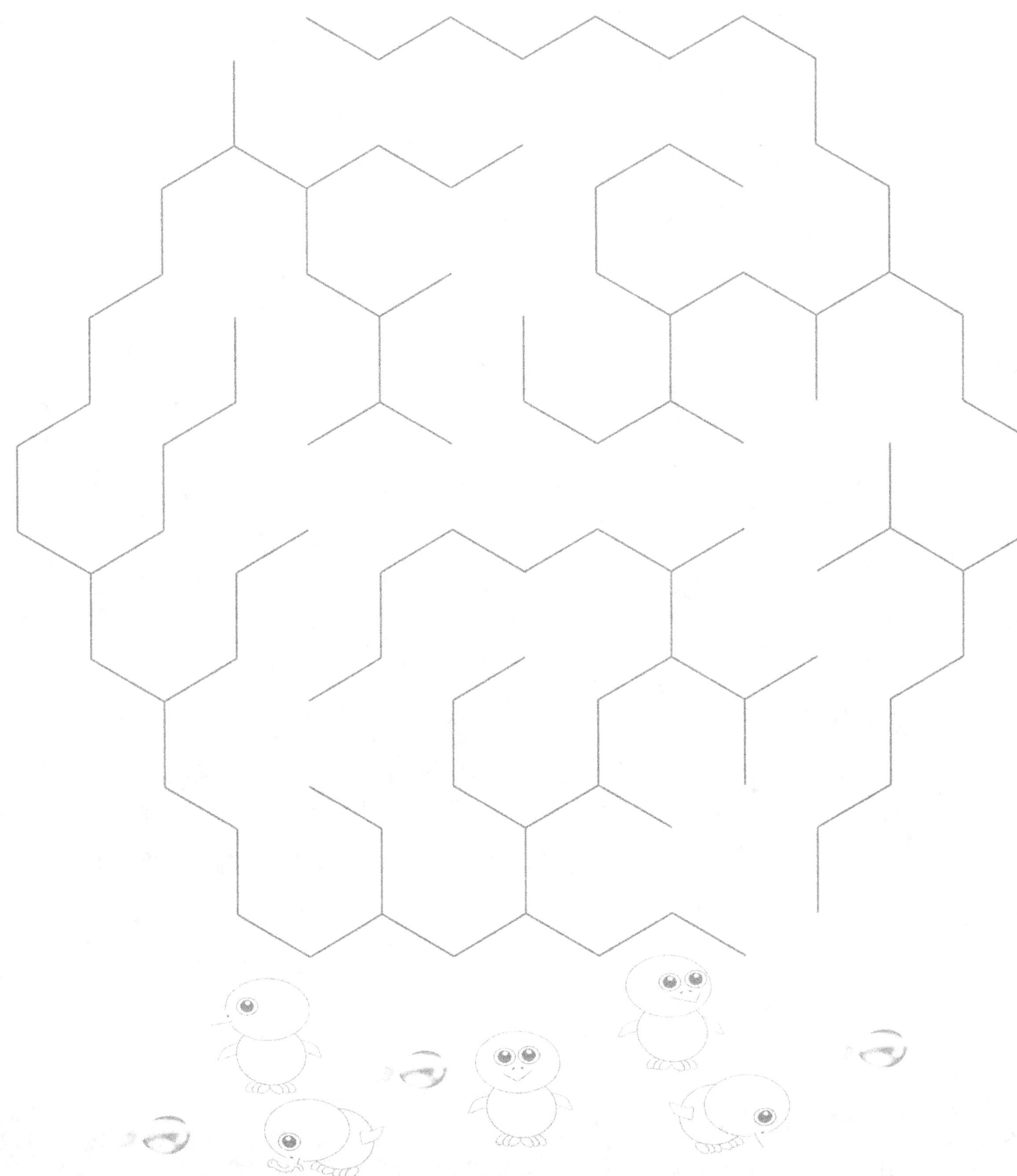

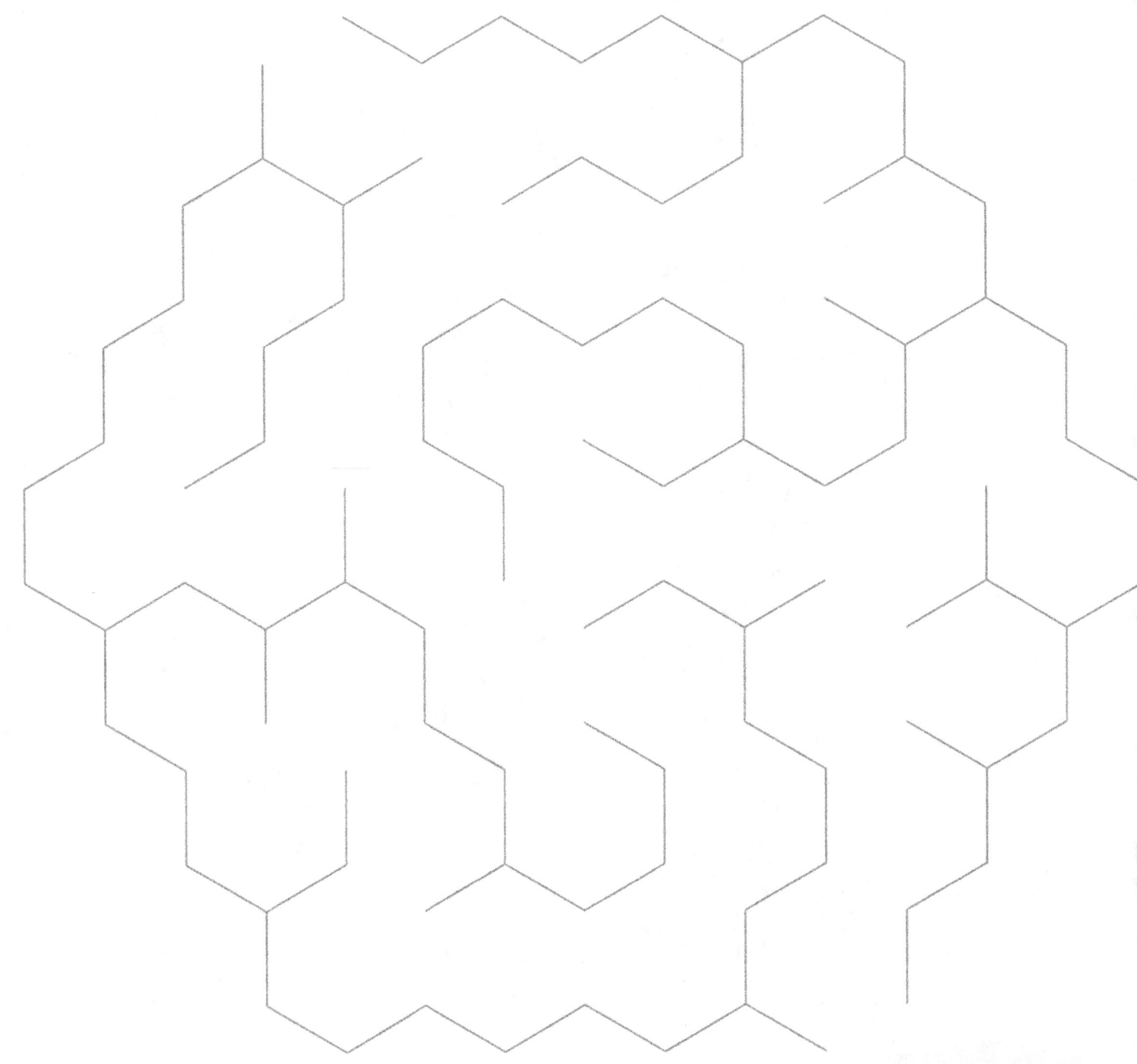

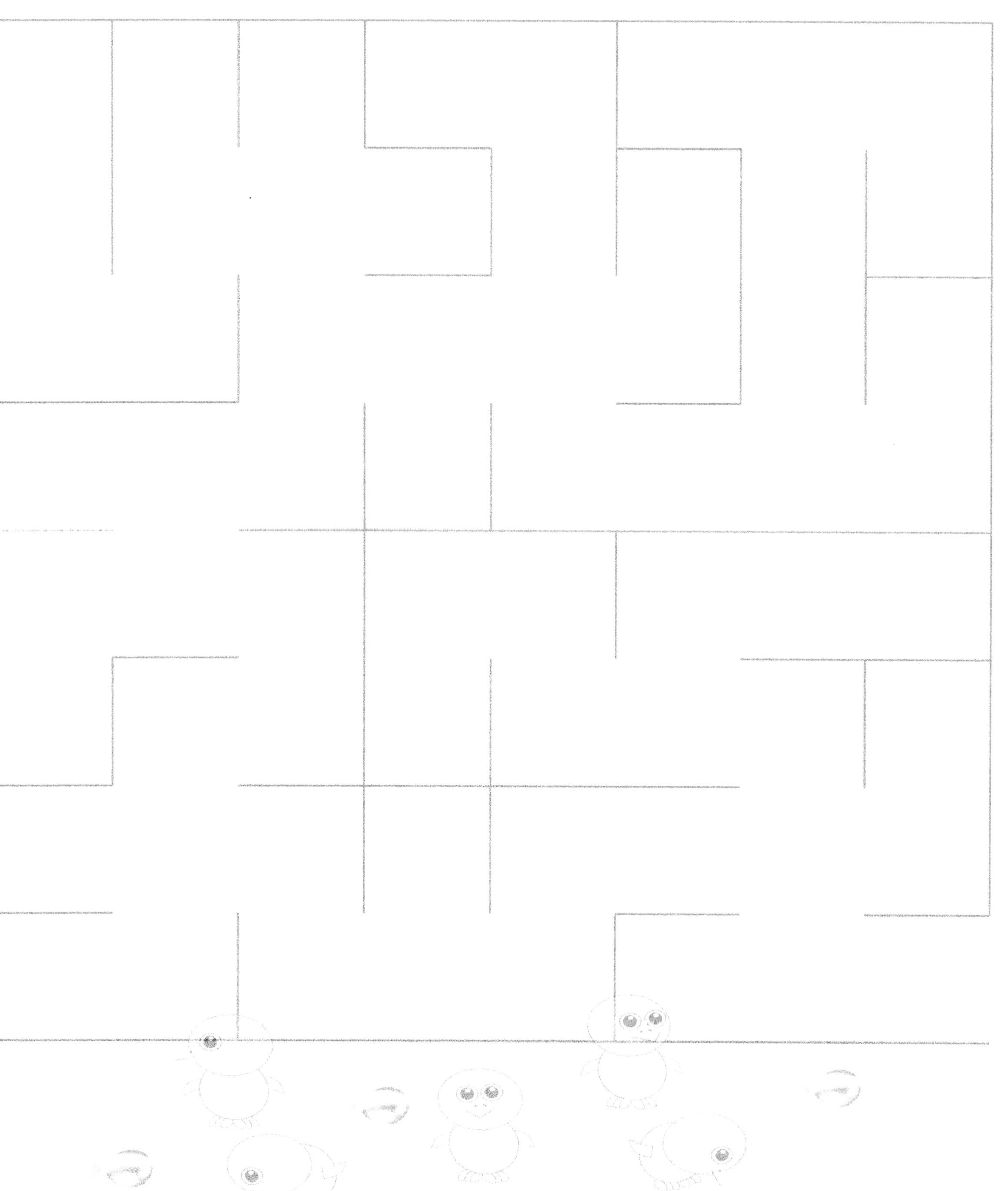

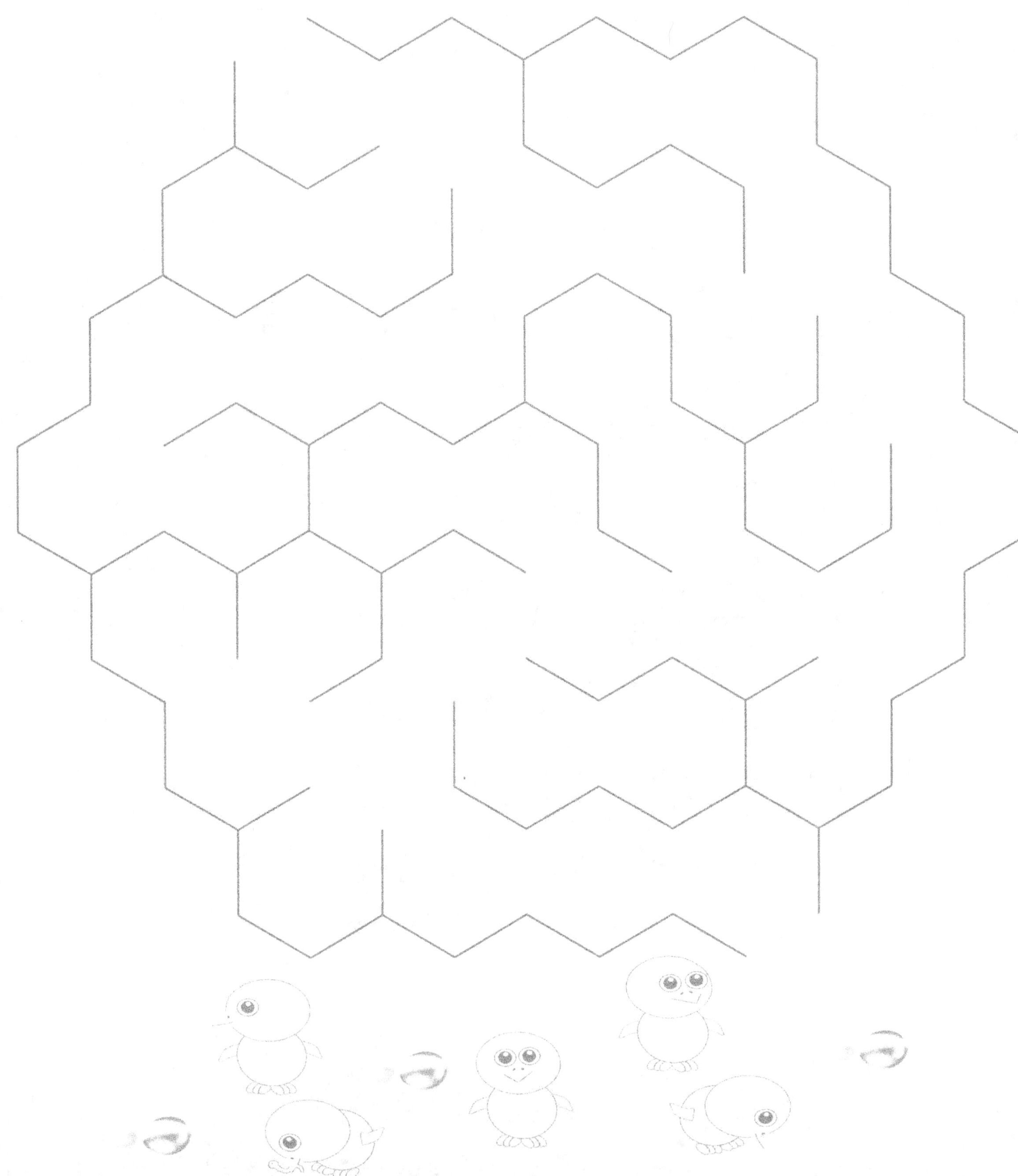

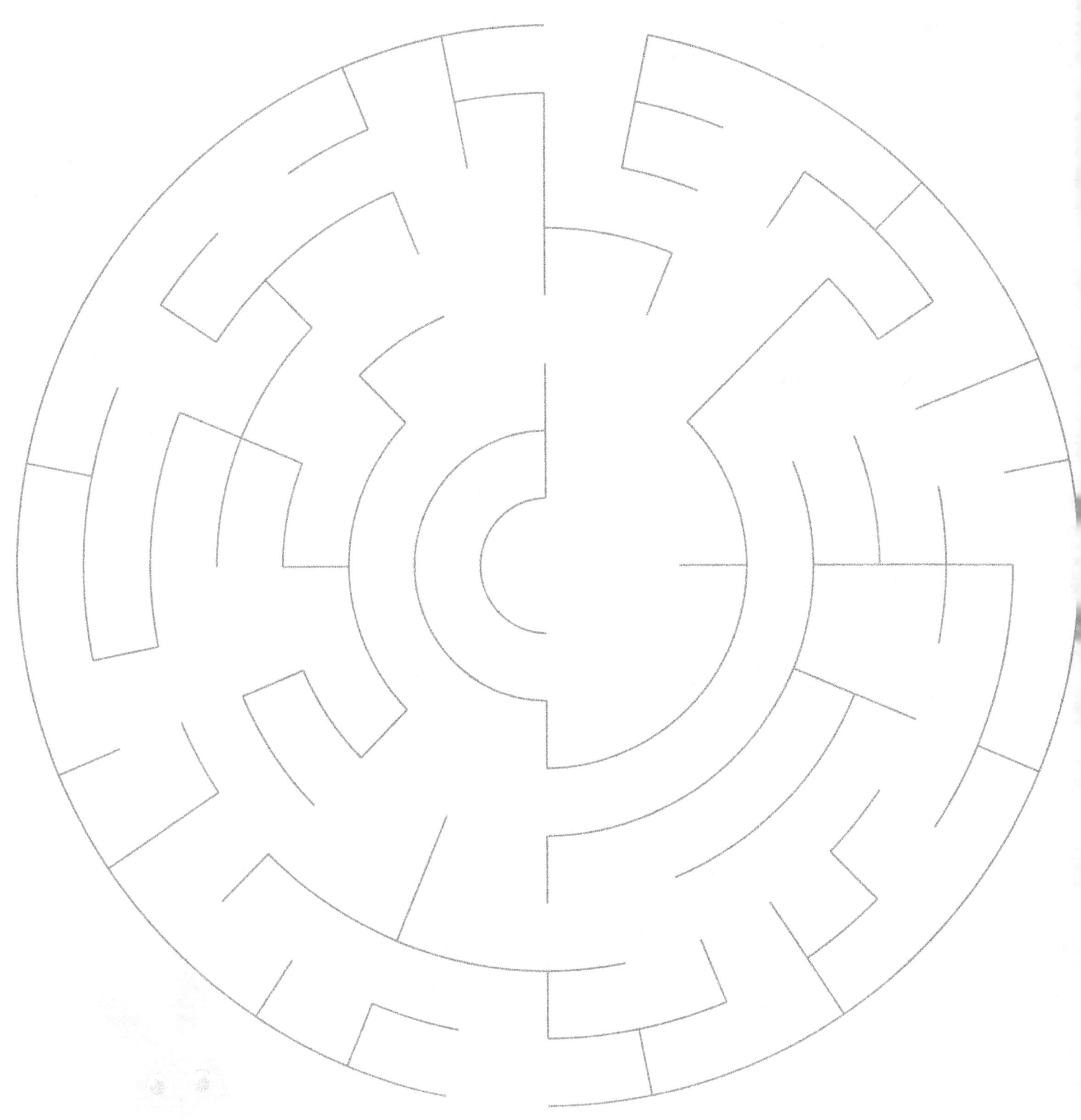

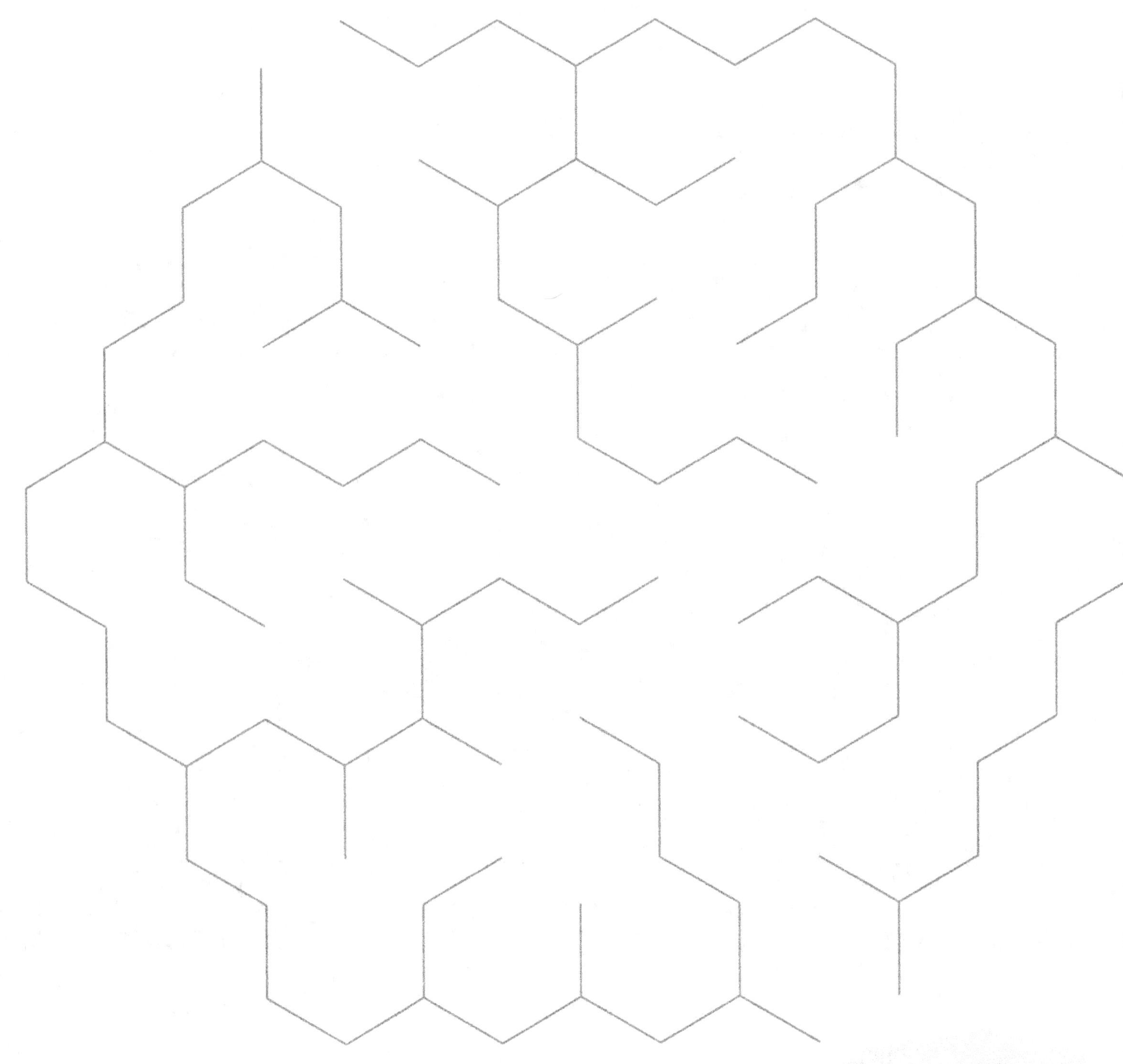

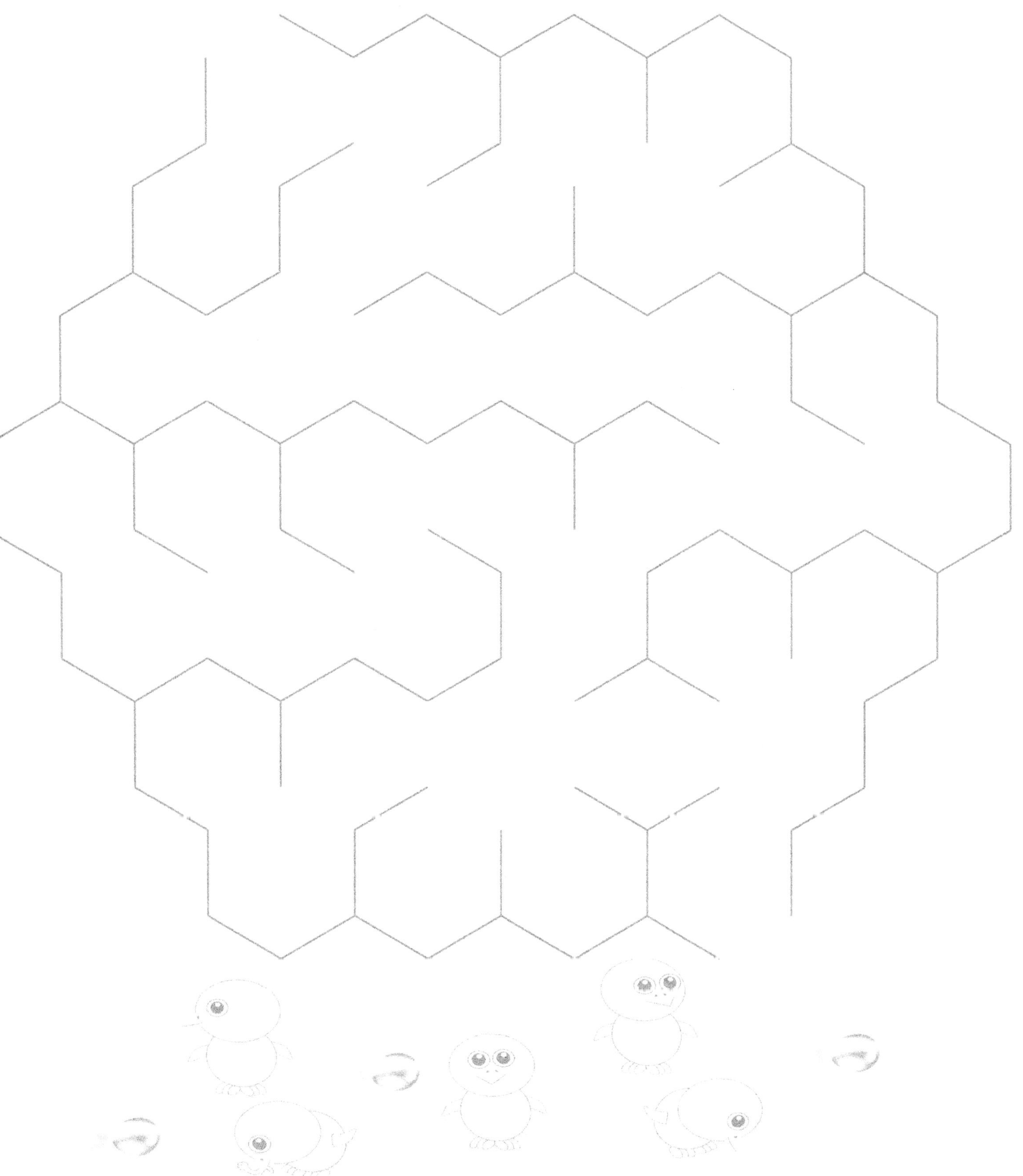

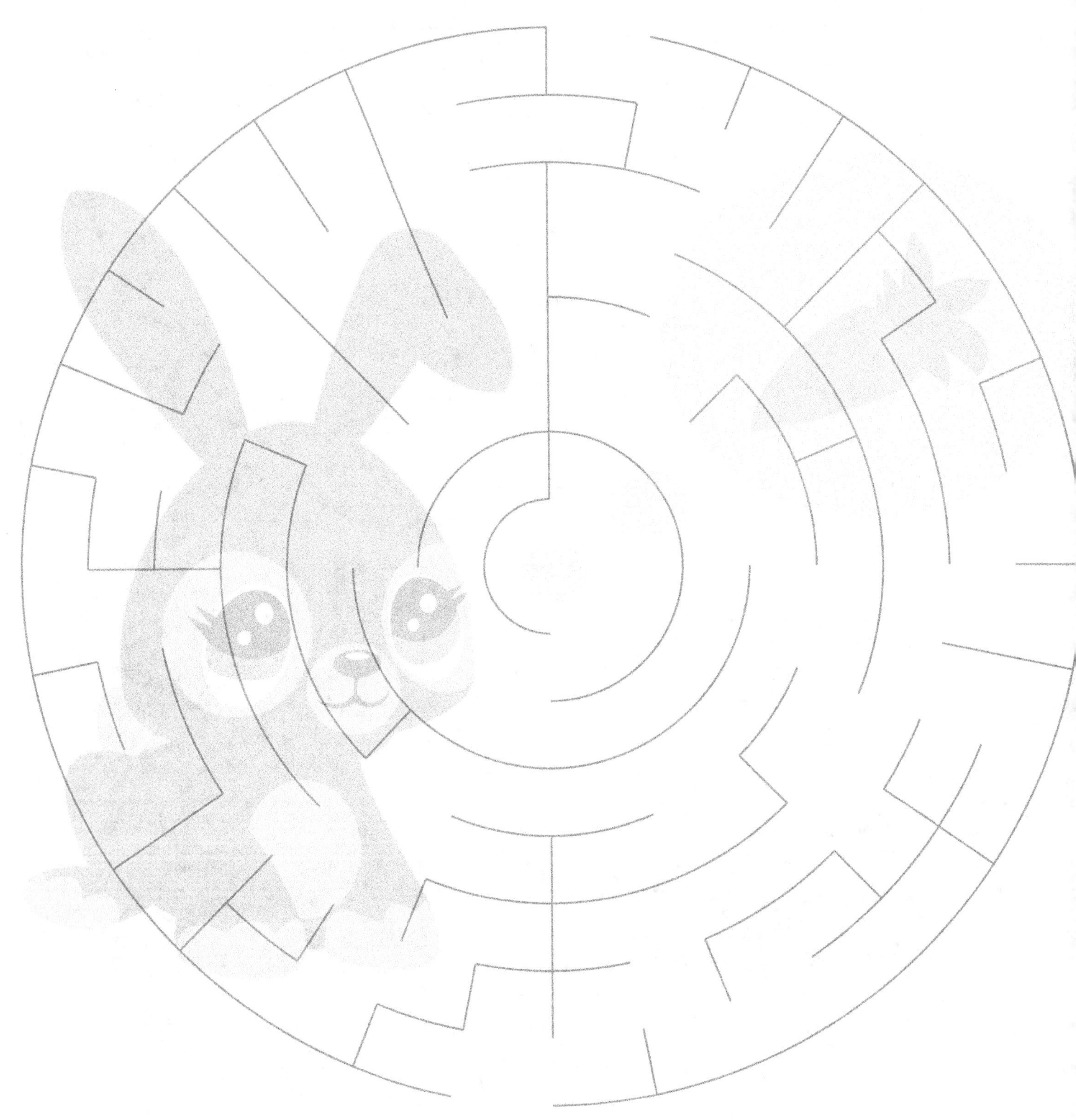

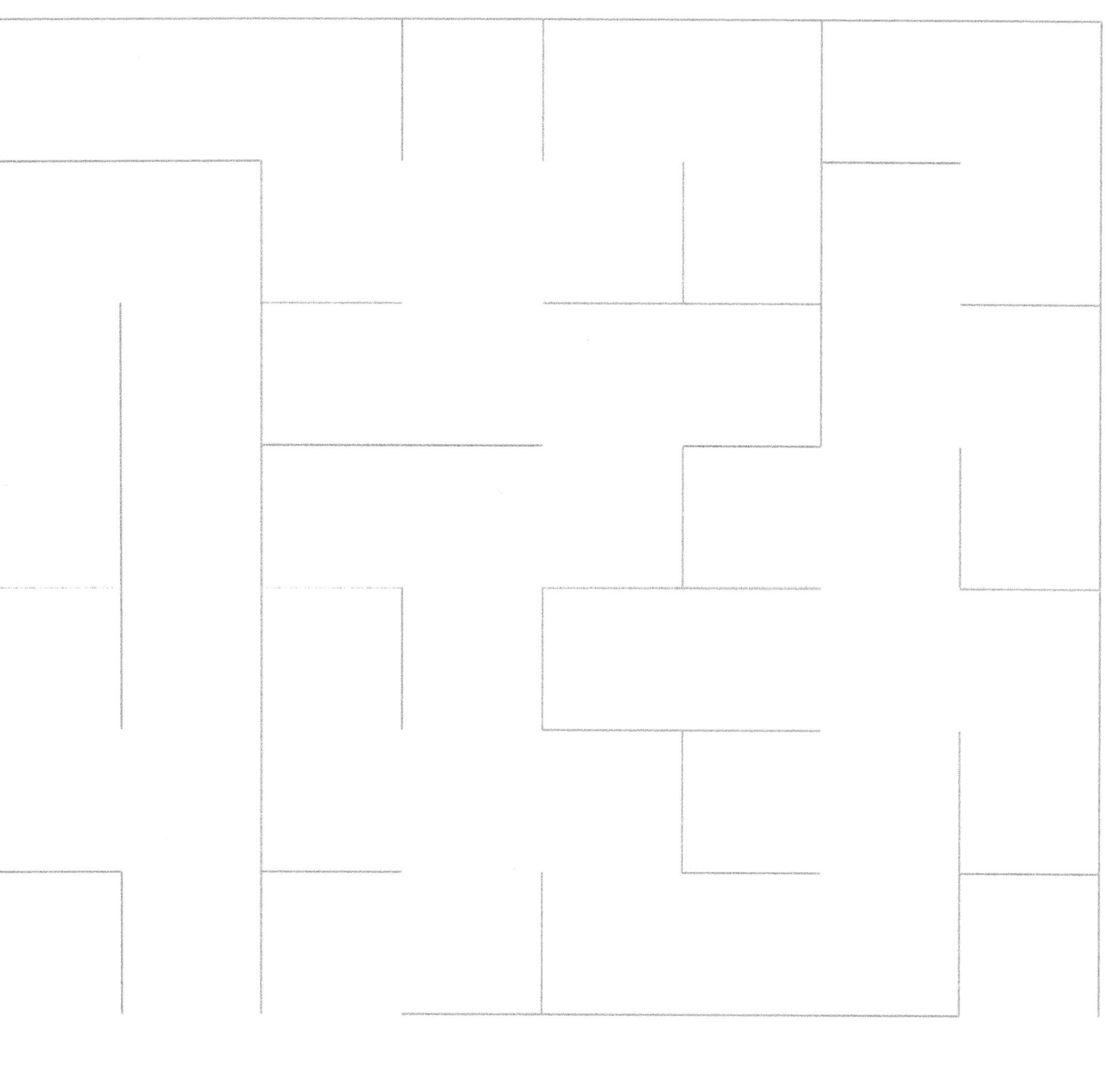

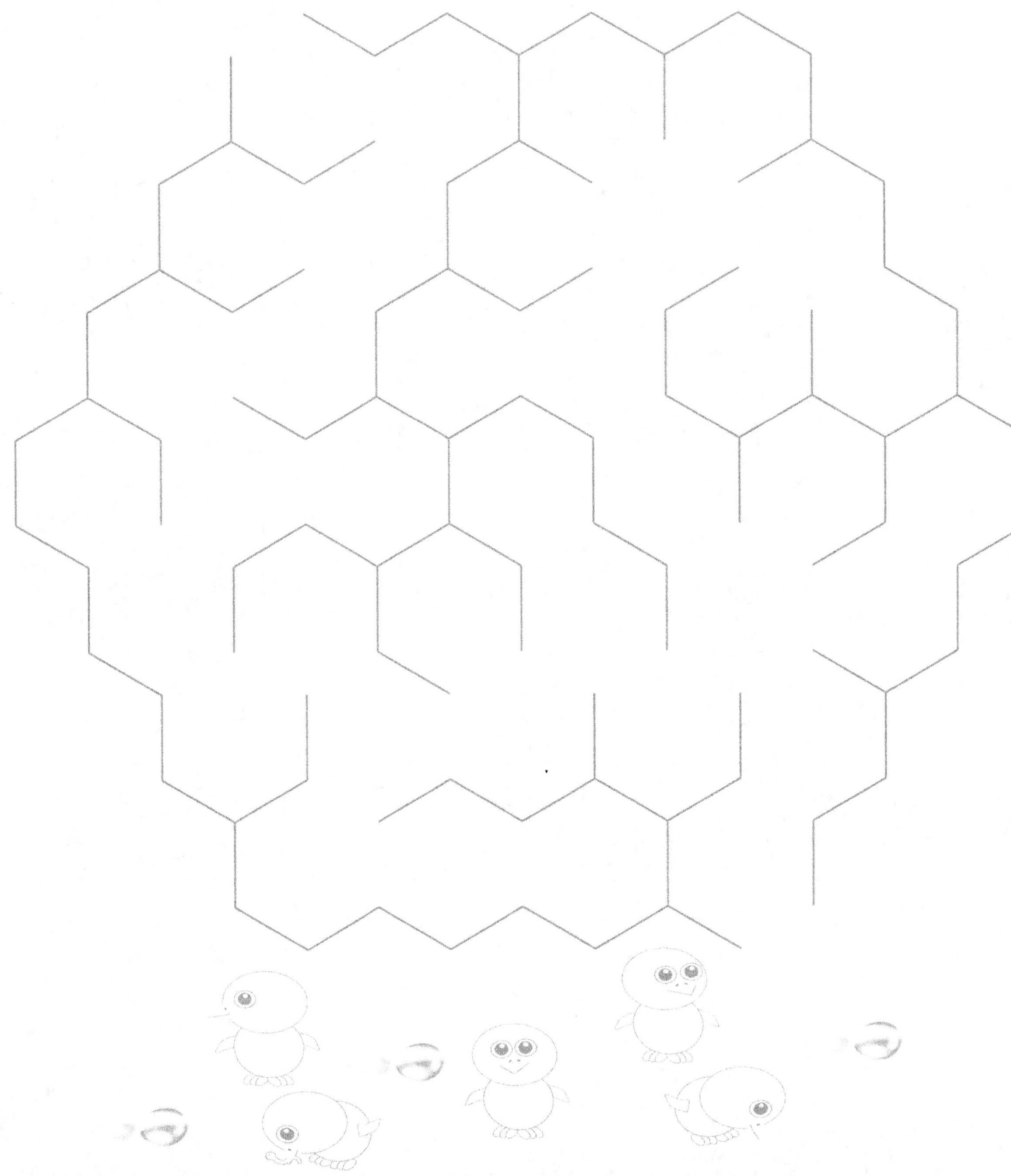

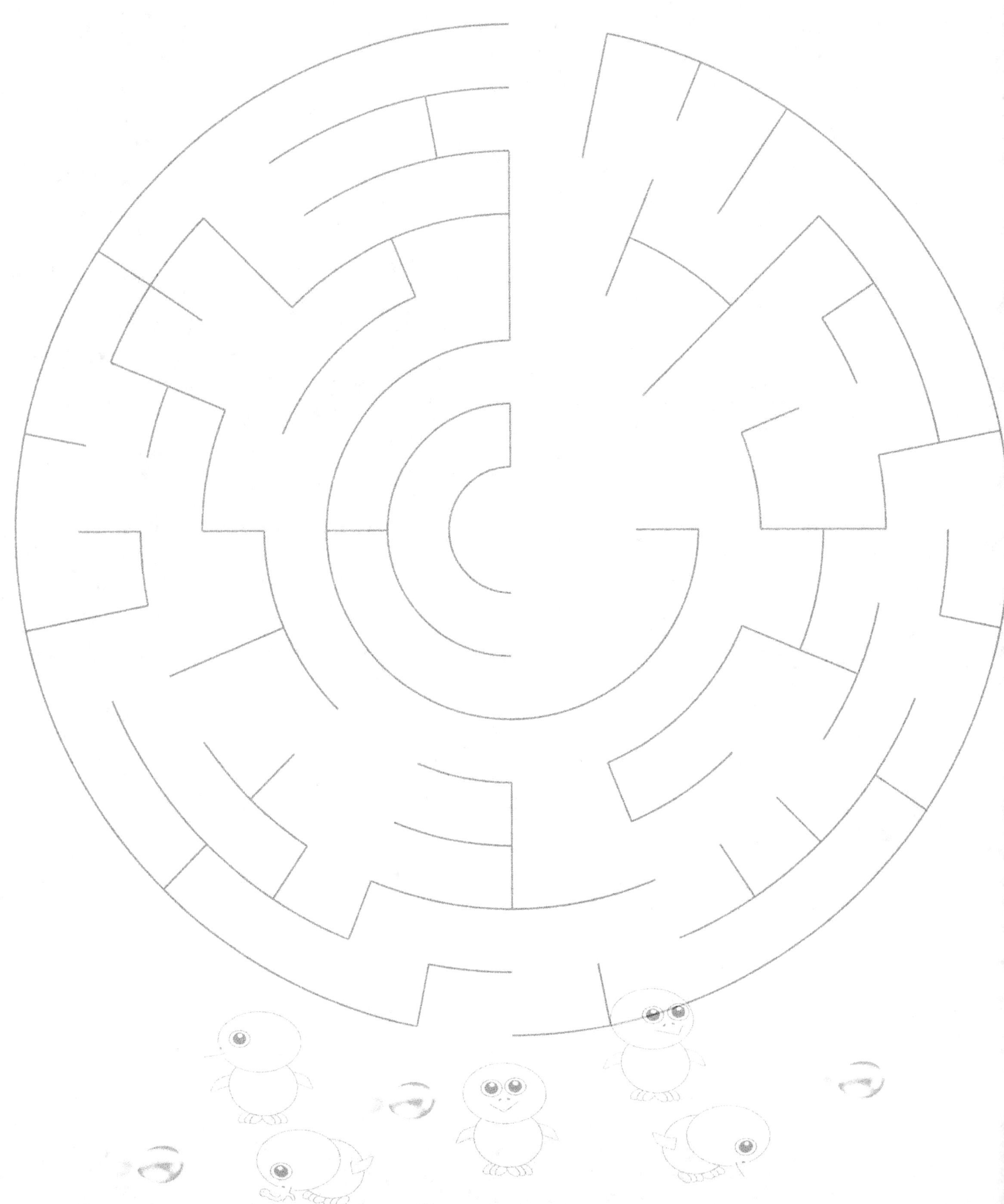